WHAT EVERY GARDENER SHOULD KNOW ABOUT EARTHWORMS

By Dr. Henry Hopp

FACTS ABOUT EARTHWORMS

With the exception of brief sections by Dr. Douglas Taff on earthworms' effects on soil nutrients, this report is by Henry Hopp, formerly with the United States Department of Agriculture and without doubt the world's leading authority on earthworms. The Department set him to the study of earthworms because of the many inquiries they were getting about the characteristics and values of these creatures. He digested all the previous work in this field, and then embarked on some experiments of his own.

We went to Dr. Hopp to get an authoritative account, in terms of the layman, on the work he and others have done.

The facts about worms are important for anyone who does composting or wishes to have better soil for farm or garden. You will find that his studies have made Dr. Hopp an enthusiast about earthworms, albeit with a scientist's caution about claims that cannot be experimentally proved. In reading his account it should be kept in mind that what the worms do in the soil essentially is what they also do in the compost pit. You will wish to encourage the maximum earthworm population in either, after reading Dr. Hopp's absorbing report.

EVERY FARMER and gardener is aware that earthworms occur widely in agricultural soil. They are especially frequent in the richer soils, although they also occur in ordinary garden or farmland. The association of earthworms with productive soil causes people to wonder if earthworms play a positive role in soil productivity or merely prefer to live in the better soils without contributing to their productivity.

This is not just an academic question. It is one that can vitally affect the productivity of many millions of acres of agricultural soil where farming or gardening is being carried on without regard to what it may be doing to the earthworm population.

There are over 3,000 species of earthworms in the world, but only a very few that are important in the tillable soils of this country. Some common ones are shown in the accompanying illustration shown opposite.

The night crawler, *Lumbricus terrestris*, is the largest of our earthworms. It is more common in the northern states. Heavy organic fertilization seems to favor its development in meadows and lawns.

Allolobophora caliginosa, with its variant known as the form *trapezoides*, is described as the common field worm. It occurs throughout the humid area of the country. It is more common than the night crawler particularly in the southern states. In the same locality, this species may prevail where the fertility level is too low for the night crawler.

On soils of extremely low fertility, neither of these species prospers. In rundown bromesedge fields around Washington, D.C., for example, the main kind is the small slim worm, *Diplocardia verrucosa*. It has no English name. There may be quite a few of them in the soil, but its holes and casts are so small that it has only a minor effect on soil properties.

Another species found quite widely in agricultural soils is the green worm, *Allolobophora chlorotica*. It is a rather short but stout worm of typical greenish color. Only because of its prevalence is this worm deserving of comment; it is actually quite inactive. Very often it is found curled up in a semi-dormant condition while the other worms are active.

Two other kinds worth mentioning are especially common in compost piles. One is the so-called manure worm, *Eisenia foetida*. It is known also as the brandling or red wriggler, the latter because of its squirming reactions when handled. This species can be told by the transverse rings of yellow and maroon which alternate the length of

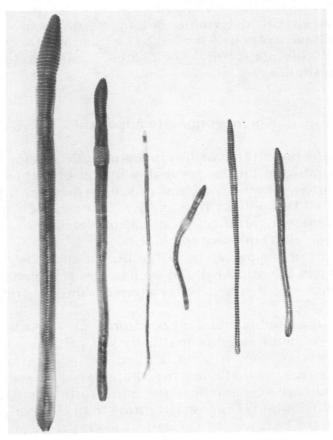

Some of the more common kinds of earthworms: from left the nightcrawler, the field worm, the Diplocardia, *the green worm, the manure worm, and the* rubellus *worm. The first four occur in farm or garden soil. The other two occur mostly in compost, but occasionally in garden soil where a large quantity of refuse has been added. Worms are pictured here 9/14ths their actual size.*

its body. The other is the stouter *Lumbricus rubellus*. It is a deep maroon color and does not have the yellow bands of the manure worm. Both these earthworms invade refuse, although the former is more prevalent in manure piles. Neither occurs commonly in agricultural land; although they will come in where large amounts of refuse are added to the soil.

In addition to these recognized species of earthworms, a so-called "hybrid" is being sold by commercial growers. It is claimed by some to be a cross between the manure worm and one of the field worms. This claim is groundless so far as we can determine. Shipments of these worms that we have examined proved to be identical taxonomically with *Eisenia foetida*. Their rates of cast production are also similar.

Where Worms Are Important

All of the important earthworms are exotic, having been introduced from Europe, probably in soil brought along with plants. However, earthworms have become widely distributed throughout the country. By now, their distribution is largely a reflection of natural variations in climate and soil from place to place.

They are more prevalent in the humid sections of the East than in the arid West. But even in desert regions they sometimes occur along water courses and in irrigated land.

Where reasonable moisture conditions prevail, their occurrence is determined primarily by soil variations. They are more common in soils derived from limestone or otherwise rich in plant nutrients, than in shale or outwash soils. Soil texture influences the earthworm population. Sandy soil contains fewer earthworms than clay soil. This is fortunate because sandy soil is likely to have good structure naturally, whereas clay soil packs together and becomes too hard for crop growth unless agencies like earthworms are present to keep the soil granulated.

Another cause of variation in their distribution is the quantity and quality of organic matter found in the soil.

4

Earthworms require both organic debris and mineral soil for food. Organic compounds satisfy their need for carbon as well as nitrogen. Carbon is normally supplied in the form of starches or sugars while nitrogen is furnished by amines and proteins. Neither nitrate nor ammonium, which are common nitrogenous compounds used to fertilize plants, can satisfy an earthworm's nitrogen budget. Proteins and amines represent only a small fraction of the total organic matter in soil while at the same time protein comprises 72% of an earthworm's dry weight. Obviously for any earthworm population to survive, there must be a quantity of available nitrogen to be ingested, digested and resynthesized into worm protein. When physical parameters such as soil texture, moisture, and temperature are suitable for optimal growth, the availability of a nitrogenous food supply becomes the ultimate factor limiting population.

In a deciduous forest, where a constant leaf fall takes place every autumn, the earthworm population is regulated by the quantity of leaves which fall and their nitrogen content. The same factor regulates the populations found in prairies and grasslands. The earthworm population will rise above its steady state limit only when organics are continuously imported into an ecosystem. Each time a gardener works compost into his soil he is raising the soil's carrying capacity and ultimately the earthworm population.

These variations in food supply, climate, and soil result in large differences in the size of the earthworm populations. There are differences in the size of the population regionally, due to climate, and locally due to the texture and origin of the soil. There may even be differences in the population from one field to the next on the very same soil due to the method of cropping the land. Hence an actual examination of your soil is the surest way of knowing whether you are in a locality where earthworms are important.

Such an earthworm examination of your soil can be made quickly. Select an area with ample vegetation on it, such as covercrop, clover, grass, etc. The examination can be made at any season of the year, although easiest during the humid period of the year. Dig out a square of earth about one foot across to a depth of approximately seven inches. Count all the earthworms you can find in this sample. Include both mature and young ones. Our experience has given us a fairly reliable thumb rule for judging the earthworm population. If a soil contains at least ten earthworms in such a sample, the population is large enough to be significant in the structural properties of the soil. Sometimes there are only one or two earthworms in the sample. This indicates that the earthworms are playing little if any real part in the physical condition of the soil.

It was once thought that earthworms are confined to occasional pieces of rich ground. This is now known to be false. Of course, there are more earthworms in the richer soils. But even ordinary garden or farmland may contain a surprisingly large population. Some idea of the number of earthworms that occur in different sections and how the number can vary may be seen from Table 1. The values are fairly representative of ordinary soil where cover is present.

Table 1
Earthworms at various locations.

Location	Earthworms to a 7-inch depth Per Square Foot (Number)	Per Acre (Number)
Marcellus, N.Y.	38	1,600,000
Geneva, N.Y.	28	1,200,000
Ithaca, N.Y.	4	190,000
New Brunswick, N.J.	28	1,200,000
Frederick, Md.	50	2,200,000
Beltsville, Md.	8	350,000
Morgantown, W. Va.	28	1,200,000
Zanesville, Ohio	37	1,600,000
Coshocton, Ohio	5	220,000
Wooster, Ohio	30	1,300,000
Holgate, Ohio	14	600,000
Lansing, Mich.	13	570,000
Dixon Springs, Ill.	20	870,000
LaCrosse, Wisc.	39	1,700,000
Mayaquez, P.R.	6	260,000

What Worms Do For Soil

The newest studies have amply demonstrated that earthworms *do* have very important effects on the productivity of soil. By no means are they just passive denizens of the soil without effect on its properties. Quite the contrary, controlled experiments now show that some of the important properties of certain kinds of soil are directly attributable to the activity of the earthworms, and that when the earthworms are absent these properties are altered.

Unfortunately, there has been a very large amount of misunderstanding about what earthworms do for the soil. Just as there are some individuals who, oblivious to the facts, stick to the old idea that earthworms are without any real importance in farm soil, there are others who, over-enthusiastically, proclaim the earthworm a cure-all for every soil trouble. Both these extreme attitudes are wrong. There are many conditions that affect the productivity of soil, and earthworms change only certain of these conditions. A clear understanding of the role of earthworms requires, therefore, a clear understanding of what makes soil productive.

The ability of soil to produce bountiful crops depends primarily on (a) a supply of moisture in the soil, (b) an adequacy of air spaces for root development, (c) available nutrients. If any of the six macronutrients (nitrogen, phosphorous, potassium, calcium, magnesium and sulfur) or eight micronutrients (manganese, iron, chlorine, copper, zinc, cobalt, boron and molybdenum) is absent from the soil, or if one of the other two productivity requirements is missing, crop growth will be poor. However, no absolute values can be established for these factors, since crops vary in their minimum requirements.

The above requirements are, basically, all that have to be considered in measuring the productivity of a soil. That is why crops can be grown only by the use of water, essential minerals, and a coarse medium, such as sand or

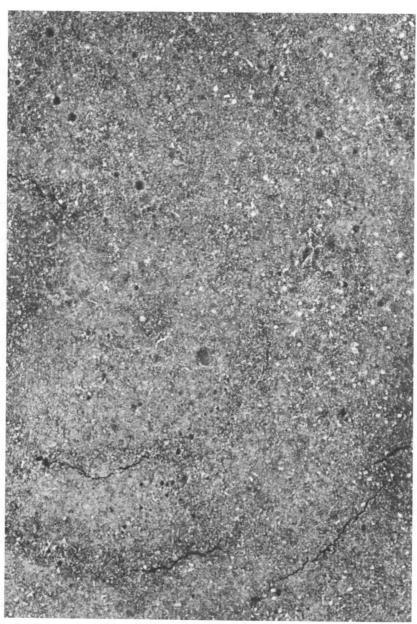

What worms do to soil: The soil at left without worms *is compact. That at right* with worms *is granulated. Note the numerous oval casts in the ground. These are highly important for good structure*

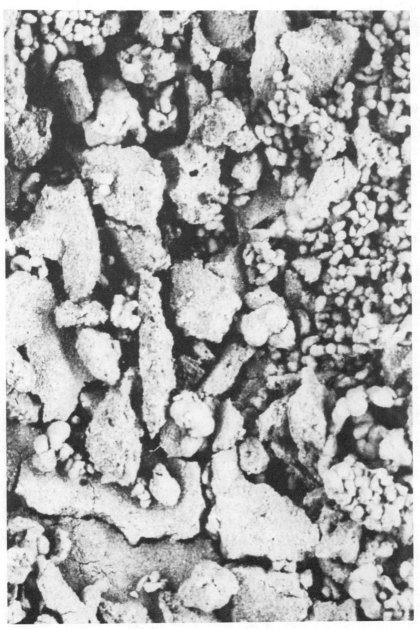

in soil, because they keep their identity when they become wet. Soil that is compact or that slumps into a compact condition is unproductive for crop growth.

gravel. Organic matter, earthworms or any of the other multitudinous considerations that go into the tilling of ordinary soil, are not necessary in hydroponic cultures.

But ordinary land is no such ideal medium for crops. Natural soil is usually deficient in one or another of the three basic requirements and sometimes these deficiencies become more acute due to cropping. So, in most soils, to provide the three basic requirements, the farmer has to adopt corrective measures. Much of soil management science has to do with the discovery of measures that correct the deficiencies in the different kinds of soils where one or more of the basic requirements is limiting the crop growth. Thus, where moisture is limiting, the farmer may irrigate; or he may use a system that lets more of the rain into the ground so that not as much is lost by runoff; or he may increase the depth or capacity of the root zone to hold water. Where aeration is poor, such as in compact clay soils, he cultivates and may use other measures for increasing the volume of large holes in the root zone; or where poor aeration is due to an overabundance of water, he may bed or drain the land. Where sufficient nutrients are lacking, he uses mineral fertilizers; or he may grow legumes that bring nitrogen into the soil from the air; or he may supply missing nutrients in manure or other organic debris that he brings onto the land.

All these measures, and others too, are adopted by gardeners and farmers because soils, as they actually exist on our lands, are not perfect media for the particular crops grown. Yet no one of these corrective measures is absolutely indispensable. There are usually several alternative ways of accomplishing the same basic purpose. However, some of the measures are practical while others may be possible only theoretically.

Earthworm activity is not one of the three basic requirements for plant growth. Rather, it comes into the category of factors which can be used to correct deficiencies in these basic requirements. Like any of the other corrective measures, earthworm activity is not indispensable. But, on some soils, it is difficult to find other practical means of doing those things which are normally done by the earthworms.

Effect on Soil Moisture

Soil that consists of coarse particles, such as sand, usually absorbs water readily. But most soil is not of this kind. Our principal kinds of agricultural soil consist of finer particles, such as silt and clay loam. Unless modified by secondary agencies, the particles pack together and become almost impervious to water. Then most of the rain runs off the surface instead of entering the soil. When soil gets into this condition, the crops suffer from drought even though the location may be one where there is adequate normal rainfall.

The intake of water by fine soil is dependent for the most part on the presence of extraneous channels. Earthworms are highly effective in making such channels. They form an interconnected web of channels which allow rain water to penetrate quickly throughout the topsoil layer. Opposite see what happened to water in a silt loam soil with and without earthworms. The water found its way between the soil particles only slowly, but ran down the earthworm channels quickly. As a result, the soil without worms had an initial absorption rate of 0.2 inches of rainfall per minute. The same soil, worked by earthworms for a period of one month, had an initial absorption rate of 0.9 inches of rainfall per minute, a fourfold improvement. The soil had about the same total capacity for rainwater, whether worms were present or not; but when earthworms were absent, the rate of intake was so slow that most of the water ran off.

The activity of earthworms is just one of several factors that increase the water-absorbing ability of soil. Mulch, compost and the roots of sod plants likewise increase infiltration. Table 2 shows how these various factors interacted to give the maximum rate of water absorption in an outdoor test on clay soil. In this test, sod and mulch were established both with and without earthworms. Two years after initiation of the test, infiltration measurements were made. Without any cover or earthworms, the soil re-

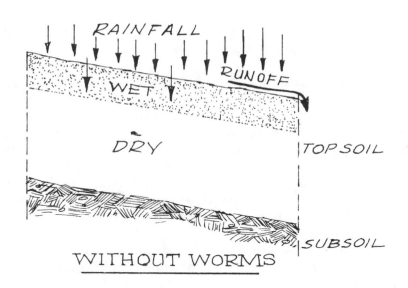

RAINFALL

RUNOFF

WET

DRY

TOPSOIL

SUBSOIL

WITHOUT WORMS

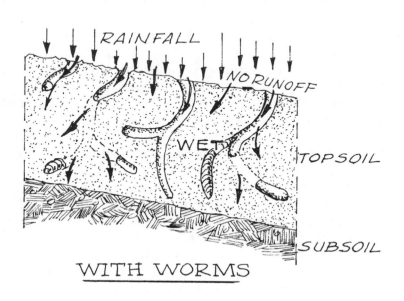

RAINFALL

NO RUNOFF

WET

TOPSOIL

SUBSOIL

WITH WORMS

mained in its original impervious condition. Addition of earthworms was without effect because the earthworms died for lack of food. Sod alone increased the infiltration rate somewhat. But when earthworms were added too, a really large improvement occurred. The soil then became highly permeable. The earthworms used the organic matter furnished by the sod and mulch for food, and by their activity made a network of channels that allowed the ready entry of water. These data indicate that the earthworms had more effect on infiltration than the sod or mulch alone.

Table 2
The influence of earthworms, sod, and mulch on the infiltration capacity of a clay soil.

| | Relative rate of infiltration | |
| | Without earthworms | With earthworms |
Cover	(inches/Minute)	(inches/Minute)
None	0.0	0.0
Fertilized sod	0.2	0.8
Mulch	0.0	1.5

When we consider all the different kinds of soil, we find that the infiltration rate depends on several different factors. So it is not possible to attribute the infiltration rate to any single factor. However, in general, there is a close association between the infiltration rate and the number of earthworms. Rarely does one find soil with a large earthworm population that does not take water fairly rapidly. Likewise, soil with few earthworms usually takes water slowly, though there are exceptions where some of the other factors besides earthworms are effective in keeping the soil open.

As might be expected, the number of earthworms in the soil follows rather closely the amount of runoff and erosion. Soil that does not erode retains its organic matter and this provides food for earthworms. Conversely, the more earthworms there are in the soil, the better the intake and less the runoff. And erosion cannot occur unless there is runoff. Table 3 shows how the size of the earthworm population tends to follow rates of runoff and erosion. The association is not exact since other factors also enter into the picture. But the association is close enough to suggest that a high earthworm population is desirable in decreasing erosion and runoff.

Table 3
Earthworms, erosion, and runoff in comparable plots
at Ithaca, N.Y.*

Treatment for the prior 10 years	Earthworms per acre (Thousands)	Erosion annually (Tons/acre)	Runoff annually (Inches/acre)
Continuous	0	30	1.77
Three-year rotation . . .	94	5	.40
Continuous meadow .	314	0	.18
Idle	813	0	.29

* Erosion and runoff data are 10-year averages; information supplied by Dr. John Lamb, Jr.

Effect on Aeration

You have probably noticed how poorly crops grow if the soil is compact. Growth is poor because there are not enough large air spaces in the soil. Not only is the absorption of rain water slow, resulting in its loss by runoff, but also aeration of the soil is deficient. Crops make their best growth where there are large spaces for the roots to grow in. Roots do not grow well in solid soil; they grow primarily in the spaces between the soil particles.

Earthworms are one of the most effective agents for loosening and aerating the soil. Their burrows make large passageways for the roots to grow in. They perforate the topsoil especially and gradually penetrate the subsoil, opening it for root growth and depositing organic matter in it (page 18). But even more important is the granulation of the soil which they bring about. This is done by their production of casts from the soil and organic debris that they eat. As the soil becomes granulated with casts, it gets looser and looser. These casts are clearly visible in any soil inhabited by earthworms (below). During damp seasons of the year, cast production is especially prolific. At that time, casts are even deposited on the surface of the ground. However, there are always many more casts underground than there are on top.

The casts are distributed for the most part in the topsoil layer. As a matter of fact, much of the dark, granular material so characteristic of topsoil often proves, on close examination, to be earthworm casts. The dark color is due to the admixture of organic matter, or humus, with the mineral material. This mixing process takes place inside the earthworms' bodies.

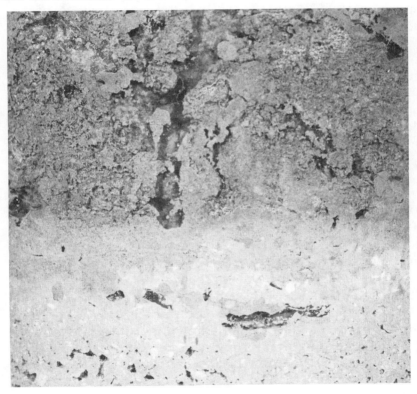

Earthworms gradually deepen the layer of topsoil and put it into productive condition. The lower part of this picture is clay subsoil. Earthworms have started to penetrate it with channels, which are lined with their humus-rich casts. The upper soil has been converted to dark-brown topsoil completely riddled by worms.

The rate of cast production depends mainly on the size of the earthworm. Large species produce a greater quantity of casts than small species, and mature ones a greater quantity than young ones. An approximate rule is that earthworms produce their own weight of casts per day. This rule is based on careful measurements in controlled tests. Transposed onto a field basis, and using data from a large number of examinations in the North Atlantic and North Central states, it appears that the average quantity of soil converted into casts amounts to about 700 lbs. per acre for each day's activity. This rate of activity holds in the damp periods of the year only; for earthworms become dormant as the soil becomes dry. Assuming days of such weather, earthworms would ingest 105,000 lbs. of soil, or more than 5% of an acre plow layer per year.

It has been mistakenly assumed that the loosening of soil by earthworms has the same kind of effect on soil as cultivation with tillage implements. Some people even think there is a controversy between earthworms and the plow. This is an unfortunate misconception. They do not do the same job. From the viewpoint of simply loosening soil, tillage implements are much more effective than earthworms.

If the soil is run down, it does not stay loose after tillage. With the first rains, the clods clump together and the loose condition made by tillage is lost. Thus, tillage gives the soil only a start with good structure (besides, of course, killing the weeds), but the ability of the soil to remain loose depends upon the properties of the soil itself. This property is known as water-stability.

Soil scientists know that the water-stability of soil is one of its most important physical characteristics. They have, therefore, given much attention to learning how soil acquires this property and they have developed precise tests to measure it. They now know that water-stability comes from the cementing of the soil particles together by sticky materials. These materials, once dried, do not redissolve in water. They are produced by the life in the soil, such as earthworms and certain micro-organisms. It is in this respect that the type of granulation produced by earthworms differs so greatly from the type produced by tillage implements.

The effectiveness of earthworms for increasing the water-stability of soil is one of their most valuable attributes. This is shown by the data in Table 4. The soils were incubated, both with and without earthworms for periods of one week. Then, each soil sample, including the casts, was given a water-stability test. Consistent increases in water-stability occurred in the samples containing earthworms, as compared with the same soil incubated for the same length of time without earthworms.

Table 4

The effect of earthworms in one week on the water-stability of soil taken from different places, as found in controlled laboratory tests.

Soil Type	Description of Soil	Water-Stability of the Soil Without Earthworms (Per cent)	With Earthworms (Per cent)
Evesboro loamy sand	Eroded bank	2.5	14.4
	Same, with organic debris added	12.9	32.3
	Another eroded bank, with organic debris added	6.6	15.0
	Abandoned brushy field	18.2	45.5
Sunnyside fine sandy loam	Eroded field, with organic debris added	4.7	10.3
	Clover meadow	73.2	79.5
Leonardtown silt loam	Eroded bank	1.3	4.8
	Same, with organic debris added	4.2	8.4
	Young hardwood forest	74.8	80.4
Christiana silt loam	Lespedeza meadow	4.5	15.7
Paulding clay	Continuous corn field	19.8	24.5
	Rotation corn field	31.1	39.2
Average of all tests		21.2	30.8

Table 5

The association of earthworms with the amount of large spaces in the soil for land in various crops, measured in the spring of the year.

Location	Condition of Land	Earthworms per Sq. Ft. (Number)	Large Spaces in the Soil (Per cent)
College Pk., Md.	Bare, following corn	2	4.0
	Young wheat following corn	6	4.2
	Meadow following wheat	22	7.4
	Continuous meadow	26	12.6
Wooster, Ohio	Bare, following corn	2	1.0
	Young wheat following corn	8	2.8
	Meadow following wheat	14	4.4
	Continuous meadow	9	8.2
Holgate, Ohio	Bare following corn	5	3.3
	Young wheat following corn	15	4.8
	Meadow following wheat	31	6.9
	Continuous meadow	38	10.7

You can easily see for yourself how earthworm casts increase the water stability of soil. Pick up a few earthworm casts from a garden either from the surface or below ground. Then select a clod that does not consist of casts and break it into pieces of about the same size as the casts. Drop some of both in water. The earthworm casts stay whole for some time while the pieces of clod quickly break apart in the water. The difference in water-stability illustrates why earthworm casts help keep soil loose when it becomes wet.

The effect of this burrowing and granulating activity is reflected under field conditions in a close association between the numbers of earthworms and the large spaces in the soil. Examples of the association are shown in the data of Table 5. These large spaces let water and air through them readily. In size, they are spaces like one finds between the grains of a coarse sand or gravel. Meadow soils averaged 10 per cent large spaces while the more compact bare land averaged only 3 per cent. In each location, their abundance followed the number of earthworms quite closely.

Is It Necessary To Plant Earthworms?

Earthworms are already widely distributed over the country and it is rarely necessary to introduce them artificially in arable land.

If there are no earthworms at all in your soil, there must be a condition that prevents them from living there. You should check into the moisture, the kind of soil, supply of organic cover, and presence of toxic chemicals to find the cause. Planting of earthworms is meaningless when there are conditions that keep the earthworms out.

Where earthworms are present but in too few number, artificial planting is not likely to have any notable effect either. Usually you need only modify the previous methods of treating the land in order to increase the population to an effective density.

On most farm and garden land, therefore, you can keep earthworm activity at a desirable level by using the correct soil management practices rather than introducing earthworms artificially.

There may be a few situations where it is desirable to raise earthworms for planting in soil or compost pits. Methods of raising earthworms for this purpose are similar to the methods used in raising earthworms for fish bait.

There has recently been considerable popular emphasis placed on introducing "hybrid" or specially-bred earthworms for soil improvement. To the best of our knowledge, there are no hybrid earthworms. Neither do we know of any artificially developed strains with special soil-building attributes not found amongst the various kinds of natural earthworms.

Building Worm Population

Earthworms are very sensitive to changes in the soil brought about by cropping the land. In localities where earthworms are present, the population varies greatly according to the farming or gardening methods used.

Recent investigations have disclosed efficient methods of maintaining earthworms on tilled land. These new practices came from studies on the life habits of earthworms.

It was found that earthworms follow a well-defined yearly cycle. One might consider the cycle as starting in the fall of the year (below). At that time, many of the earthworms are young, just starting their life. With the advent of wet, cool weather, they become extremely active physically. They feed on the organic debris in and on top of the soil, and mix it with the mineral soil to produce casts, as well as making new burrows in the soil. During damp, cool nights, and occasionally on wet cloudy days, too, they come out of their burrows to seek new areas to inhabit. Within a few hours of a night, they may migrate a considerable number of feet. With dawn, they disappear into the ground but the tracks they leave in the soft ground are evidence of their nocturnal meanderings.

The high level of physical activity normally continues throughout the fall, winter and spring. During this period, the young earthworms mature and more eggs are laid. During the winter, both mature and young earthworms, as

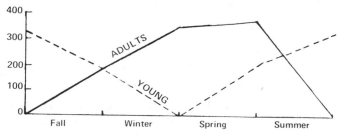

This shows the annual cycle of earthworms in sodland, data from plots of the Maryland Agricultural Experiment Station.

well as eggs, can be found in the soil. But by late spring, most of the earthworms are mature. With the coming of summer, the soil dries and heats. The earthworms become less and less active. They lay eggs and many die. During the hottest and driest part of the summer, almost all the earthworms in a garden are young ones or unhatched eggs that had been deposited by the mature ones before they died.

Thus, summer is a period of sharp decline in physical activity of the earthworms. At that time of the year they have very little effect on soil. It is mainly a period during which the generation starts for the ensuing year.

This cycle is a reflection of the seasonal changes in weather. Differences in weather from year to year or from one region to another can modify the cycle somewhat. It can be modified also by keeping the soil moist and cool during the summer through watering or mulching. The earthworms then will be physically active throughout the year. However, the natural lifecycle fully adapts earthworms to the seasonal changes in weather without their requiring such artificial help.

The main reason that earthworms decrease on tilled land is the lack of protective cover and organic debris in the winter. Their physical activity is at a maximum during this time, and to carry on their activity, they require organic debris for food. If this is lacking, they die or leave the field in search of a more hospitable area.

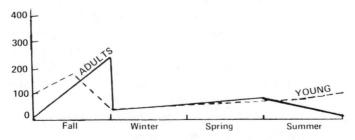

Earthworm cycle in a cornfield: Most of the earthworms are killed in the late fall or early winter, and they do not build back again fully until the following fall.

21

In the northern section of the country, where the soil usually freezes during the winter, there is one other provision that must be made for the earthworms. They must be protected against freezing temperatures in the late fall. Earthworms change with the season in their resistance to cold. During the summer, they would die if they were subjected to freezing temperature. But by winter they are fully able to live in soil that is actually frozen. However, this change in tolerance develops only slowly. In the vicinity of Washington, D.C., the earthworms do not usually develop resistance to freezing temperatures until late December.

On land protected with sod or other debris, the soil temperature drops slowly as the cold weather of winter sets in. Bare ground, on the contrary, is subject to violent fluctuations in temperature. One or two days of low temperature in the late fall may freeze bare ground, especially at night, while soil under sod, protected by the insulative cover of leaves and litter, does not freeze. Under sod, then, the earthworms have sufficient time to adapt themselves to the freezing temperatures of winter, while on bare ground they may be killed before developing cold resistance.

An example of the drastic effect that freezing weather in the fall has on the earthworms in unprotected ground was observed around Washington in 1946. In two days of subfreezing temperature at the start of December, two-thirds of the earthworms on tilled land were killed by freezing. This decline is shown (see chart) by the sharp drop in mature worms at the start of the winter.

To protect the earthworms from freezing in the late fall, almost any kind of insulation is satisfactory. Manure, compost, chopped corn stover, wheat straw, a cover crop such as ryegrass which gives a heavy sod, or a mulch of dead grass and weeds make suitable protective coverings (opposite). Such materials are at the same time a source of organic food for the earthworms over winter.

Unprotected soil becomes clumped. It has few large spaces for aeration and water intake and when it dries, it hardens. This condition is due to the destructive action of frost on the wet soil.

Soil worked by earthworms, on the contrary, stays loose and granular. The numerous channels let water enter quickly and provide spaces for the roots to grow luxuriantly. Frost cannot damage it because the earthworm channels drain out excess water.

Soil can often be improved a great deal in just a single winter by protecting the earthworms. The degree of improvement attainable is shown by tests conducted in Ohio and Maryland. Land that had been cropped to corn in a three-year rotation was selected for the tests. In the late fall, after the corn had been harvested and the wheat had become established, some of the land was left uncovered and some was covered with mulch. The following spring the condition of the soil and the earthworm population were measured.

The effect of the treatment was shown by comparing the covered land with the uncovered land and with adjacent sod land. Table 6 gives the data. Without protection over winter, the tilled land was in much poorer condition than the sod. Covering the tilled land overcame much of the difference. The infiltration and earthworm population were as favorable as in sod, and the volume of large spaces was almost as good. Water-stability was still below that of sod land, but there was a substantial improvement from the treatment.

Table 6

Earthworms and soil physical properties in tilled land covered over winter compared with uncovered tilled land and adjacent sod land. Measurements made in the spring; average of 3 localities in Ohio and Maryland.

Soil Property	Tilled land in young wheat: Covered over winter	Tilled land in young wheat: Uncovered over winter	Sod land
Relative infiltration (In./min.)	0.31	0.10	0.36
Large spaces (Per cent)	7.0	3.9	10.5
Water stability (Per cent)	59	44	79
Earthworms (No./sq. ft.)	52	10	24

A good cover of leguminous sod established by the late fall, as in this sweet clover field, protects earthworms and gives them food over winter. Their activity improves greatly the condition of the soil during the winter.

Even inert materials, such as boards and stones, will protect the earthworms over winter, as can be seen during the winter by looking beneath them where they are lying out on bare fields. Such things are, of course, not practical for covering tilled land, although they do demonstrate the wide range of materials that can serve as protection for earthworms during the winter.

These problems pertain more to farmland than intensively cultivated garden patches, where with good use of manure, green manure, and compost, there is little difficulty in maintaining the earthworm population. But the dramatic differences which occur in farmland when protective practices are followed have both interest and significance for the small-scale grower.

When organic debris and (in the northern states) insulative cover are given the earthworms during the winter, they prosper even if the land is tilled every year. Soil so protected is well granulated and porous the following spring, in contrast to unprotected land. An illustration of this effect is shown below.

Laboratory feeding tests have shown that the larger kinds of earthworms thrive best on organic debris that contains a higher percentage of nitrogen, as in legumes, garbage and manure. See Table 7. These studies also indicate the value of adding nitrogen-rich organics to a compost pile.

This soil had been cropped continuously to corn for 7 years. Each year it was reduced to a compact condition. The photo shows how the soil now has been converted to a loose granular in one winter by protecting the worms. The earthworm casts show clearly.

When the earthworm population is increased in sod land by good agronomic practices, marked changes often take place in the soil. As has been explained previously, earthworm activity alone does not explain all the changes that result, but it does influence some of the physical characteristics of the soil. At the Ohio Agricultural Experiment Station, for example, two areas of sod, consisting of alfalfa and timothy, were differently limed. One area was limed so that the soil was almost neutral (pH 7.0). The other area was limed only slightly, so that the soil stayed rather acid (pH 5.5). Measurements in the soil revealed the following:

Soil Measurements	pH 5.5	pH 7.0
Earthworm (No./sq. ft.)	4.3	13.5
Earthworm holes (No./sq. ft.)	22	58
Relative infiltration rate, (In./minute)	0.04	0.30

The holes referred to were those appearing on a horizontal cut made 3 inches deep in the topsoil. With the heavier liming, the earthworms increased, resulting in more holes in the topsoil. The greater number of holes allowed the water to go into the soil more quickly.

Table 7

Change in body weight of the common field worm when fed different kinds of organic material together with a silt loam topsoil.

	Change in Body Weight	
Kind of Organic Material	Gain (Per Cent)	Loss (Per Cent)
Lespedeza leaf litter	21.5	
Fresh cow manure	10.7	
Green clover leaves	7.8	
Brown soybean leaves	5.6	
Dead bromesedge leaves		0.5
Weathered corn leaves		5.2
None		13.4
Wheat straw		14.1
Sawdust		18.2

Effect On Nutrients

Earthworms affect the nutrient-supplying ability of soil by taking organic debris from the surface and incorporating it into the topsoil. They digest the debris and excrete in their casts what nutrients they do not need for their own nutrition. These casts are deposited in their channels throughout the topsoil and some even in the subsoil. So distributed through the root zone, the casts constitute a source of nutrients for the vegetation. The richness of the casts depends on the kind of organic debris and mineral soil that the earthworms have for food.

Very thorough chemical analyses have been made of earthworm casts and uneaten soil by H.A. Lunt and H.G.M. Jacobson of the Connecticut Agricultural Station. They found that the casts isolated from a corn field when compared with the uneaten soil from the top six inch plow layer contained about five times the nitrate, seven times the available phosphorous, three times the exchangeable magnesium, eleven times the potassium and 1.5 times the calcium. The increases came from the corn stalks digested by the earthworms, and not from the soil ingested with the stalks.

It has been suggested that earthworms add to the nutrient content of soil by liberating chemicals in the mineral soil they eat. Until recently there hasn't been any reliable evidence to justify this idea.

The indication that worms do have a chemical effect on soil comes from the following experiment performed at Garden Way by Dr. Douglas Taff. Large plastic containers were filled with 41 pounds of dry, sandy loam soil. To the containers distilled water and known quantities of earthworms (L. rubellus) were added. Initial samples of both soil and earthworms were frozen for future analysis and the appropriate controls were run in pots containing soil but no worms. After forty days, several soil samples were taken from each experimental container. The following factors were measured: pH, cation exchange capacity, lime requirement, total nitrogen, nitrate and nitrite, ammonium, reserve phosphate, available phosphate, available calcium, available potassium, available aluminum, available magnesium, available manganese, available iron, available copper, and available molybdenum. The nutrients added to the soil by the death of a measured number of the original earthworm population were subtracted from the soil analysis to give the final results. In this manner the effect of the earthworms on the nutrient availability of a mineral soil could be determined.

Only potassium (+18.8%) and manganese (+68.2%) demonstrated increases in availability. Neither these changes nor the input of nitrogen from worms which had died during the experiment could explain, however, why there was such a spectacular increase in the soil's ability to grow annual rye grass.

Soil samples were taken from the wormless controls as well as from the experimental containers. All earthworms were removed from the latter and the soil was puddled to destroy its physical structure. Pots were then filled with the puddled samples and seeded with a known quantity of annual rye. Moisture was kept at a constant level by using double distilled water. This ensured that no extraneous nutrients would enter the test.

After two weeks under lights the rye growing in the "worm" soil was obviously thicker, taller, and more healthy looking. Chemical analysis of the leaves revealed no significant increases in the content of nitrogen, calcium or magnesium when compared to plants grown in soil derived from the wormless control. There were, however, significant gains in the total leaf phosphorous (35.6%) and potassium (51.9%) over the control samples. After four weeks of growth the differences between the quantity of green matter per pot had become less acute, but were still present. The phosphorous content of the rye had stabilized at 0.42% and the potassium content was now inversely proportional to the size of the plant because of dilution. A larger plant simply has a bigger volume. At six weeks all the pots contained equal amounts of plant matter and the potassium content had stabilized at 3.41%.

Based on these results, a person is able to argue that

earthworms in actuality do have the ability to modify mineral soil. For example, if potassium, phosphorous or other nutrients such as manganese are made more soluble by releasing them in their ionic forms, then this might partially explain the soil and leaf analysis data. Alternatively, plant nutrients might become bound in organic chelates produced by the worm. This could make them more available to a plant, but partially "invisible" to soil analysis. A third possibility exists in which earthworms produce organic compounds which are stimulatory to increased root growth. This could account for the faster growth rate and higher phosphorous and potassium content of the two-week-old rye.

Plants which germinate and grow rapidly are usually healthier and more resistant to stress. If, as has been shown with rye, you can increase a plant's rate of growth, its vigor and its chance of survival, then there appears to be an obvious agricultural reason for stimulating larger earthworm populations.

Effect On Crop Yield

Since earthworms improve several of the important properties of soil, it is only reasonable to expect better yields when earthworms are present. In general, this is true. A soil will usually yield more when a large earthworm population is present than when it has a few earthworms. This is due in part to the effect of the earthworms themselves and in part to other productivity factors that parallel changes in the earthworm population. So the number of earthworms is a useful indication of the productivity of soil.

People frequently ask how much the yield of crops is increased by earthworms. A simple, direct answer cannot be given. It varies with the condition of the soil and the kind of crop.

This is illustrated by the following greenhouse experiment. Two crops, soybeans and wheat, were planted in a silt loam topsoil that was in good structure. The soil contained a large number of earthworms to begin with and they had granulated the soil rather well. These earthworms were removed at the start of the experiment. Also the soil was fertilized heavily. Thus, the soil was put in a highly productive condition, both physically and chemically. In a second set of plantings, the good structure was destroyed by puddling and compacting the soil. A third set was likewise puddled, but earthworms were then added to restore the structure.

The results of this test are given in Table 8. The soybeans were severely retarded in the soil with poor structure; growth was only one-fifth as much as in the soil with good structure. Earthworm activity restored almost all the difference. The wheat did not suffer as much from poor structure; growth was three-quarters of that in the soil with good structure. Again, earthworms restored the productivity.

Table 8
An experiment on the importance of earthworm activity to the productivity of a silt loam soil.

| | Weight of crop plant | |
Soil and Earthworm Treatment	Soybeans (grams)	Wheat (grams)
Natural soil structure	2.96	9.5
Soil structure destroyed	0.56	7.1
Soil structure destroyed, living earthworms added	2.30	10.5

This experiment shows that earthworm activity becomes more important as the structure of the soil declines. Also, earthworm activity is more important with a crop, like soybeans, that is sensitive to soil structure. Most vegetables are very sensitive in this respect.

When the structure of a soil is very bad, the improvement in plant growth due to earthworms can be little short of amazing. The cover pictures show the effect of earthworms on the yield of hay in a red, clay loam subsoil. Both barrels were heavily fertilized, manured, limed, cultivated, and seeded. The treatments were the same except earthworms were added to the one barrel. Without earthworms there was a weak growth of vegetation, mainly grass and weeds. The average yield was at the rate of 0.6 tons of hay per acre. With earthworms, there was a luxuriant growth of ladino clover, averaging at the rate of 2.0 tons of hay per acre. The earthworms resulted in more than three times the yield, as well as a greater proportion of the highly desirable clover. Such a large amount of fine hay was particularly surprising for a soil of such low natural productivity.

In soils that have good structure—high porosity and water-stability—no yield benefits can be expected from the physical activity of earthworms. The benefit of earthworms is then confined to their chemical effects on soil.

Besides the possible solubilization of materials composing organic debris and mineral precipitates, earthworms add a large quantity of nutrients to the soil at the end of their life cycle. A population goes through seasonal fluctuations which are dependent on the climate. The young hatch in the fall and enter a period of rapid growth which continues into the following spring. During this period large quantities of nitrogenous material, normally unavailable to plants, is converted to worm protein. As the hot weather of summer approaches the adults begin to die. These in turn disintegrate by means of microbial action. This process releases large quantities of nitrogen as well as other nutrients at a time when the chemical demand on the soil is at its peak due to growing plants. Lawrence and Millar have shown that two weeks after death, 70% of the nitrogen originally trapped in worm tissue is now present in forms readily available to plants. (25% nitrate, 45% ammonium, 3% soluble organic compounds and 27% unaccounted for). For a normal earthworm population of 2,000,000 per acre, these figures translate into a yearly turnover of 20 lbs. of ammonium and 38 lbs. of nitrate. These effects are shown on the opposite page. The dead earthworms resulted in three times the yield, the living earthworms in only slightly more.

These experiments lead to the following conclusions:

(1) Earthworms help the physical condition of the soil by their activity. With poor-structured soil and crops sensi-

tive to structure, an increase in yield can be anticipated. But little or no increase in yield will result if (a) the soil has good structure naturally (b) you are growing crops that are not especially sensitive to poor structure, (c) growth is limited by a lack of other things such as nutrients or water.

(2) Earthworms help the fertility of soils by releasing nutrients from organic material and by increasing the availability of inorganic minerals. After their death, nutrients are released at a period when the maximum chemical demand is being placed on the soil by plant development. With soils of low fertility and with crops having high fertility requirements, an increase in yield can be anticipated. But little or no increase can result if (a) the soil is naturally rich, especially in organic matter, (b) you are growing a low fertility crop, (c) the earthworms were killed the previous winter by improper management practices, (d) growth is limited by lack of other things such as water or aeration.

In this crock experiment, a soil with fairly good structure was used. It was fertilized, cultivated and then treated with: left, no earthworms; center, dead worms mixed into soil; right living worms introduced. The dead earthworms resulted in three times the yield, the living earthworms resulted in only slightly more.